MY FIRST LOOK AT VEHICLES

BIG TRUCKS DO LOTS OF DIFFERENT JOBS

Trucks

CATHY TATGE

CREATIVE EDUCATION

Published by Creative Education

P.O. Box 227, Mankato, Minnesota 56002

Creative Education is an imprint of The Creative Company

Designed by Rita Marshall

Photographs by Corbis (David Keaton, Charles O'Rear, Galen Rowell), Gregory A. Fischer,

Getty Images (Stone), Richard Gross, Wernher Krutein (photovault.com), Sally McCrae

Kuyper, MackTrucks, Inc., Bonnie Sue Rauch, D. Jeanene Tiner, Unicorn Stock Photos

(B.W. Hoffmann)

Library of Congress Cataloging-in-Publication Data

Tatge, Cathy. Trucks / by Cathy Tatge.

p. cm. — (My first look at vehicles)

Includes index.

ISBN-13: 978-1-58341-530-6

I. Trucks—Juvenile literature. I. Title. II. Series.

TL230.15.T38 2007   629.224—dc22   2006027448

First edition 9 8 7 6 5 4 3 2 1

Trucks

King of the Road

Trucks are vehicles that drive on roads. They are bigger than cars and motorcycles. Trucks are the kings of the road.

A pickup truck is the smallest kind of truck. Most pickups can fit only one or two **passengers** inside. People use the back of the pickup truck to carry different things.

SOME PICKUP TRUCKS CAN DRIVE ON ROUGH GROUND

The biggest trucks on the road are called semitrailers, or semis. They are made of two pieces. The front part is the cab. This is where the driver sits. The back part is the trailer. This is the part that holds everything that the semi moves.

Trucks Long Ago

The first trucks used steam to move. Water that is very hot makes steam. Trucks that used steam could not go very far. They needed to stop for more water all the time.

Truck drivers need a

special driver's **license**

to drive a truck.

People called **engineers** wanted to make trucks that did not need water. That way, people could move things faster.

Gottlieb Daimler (*GOT-leeb DIME-ler*) was a German engineer. In 1896, he made a truck that used **gasoline** to move. It could travel farther than the first trucks. Soon, people used trucks to move many things at one time.

The biggest trucks are called
"big rigs." They can carry more
than 33,000 pounds (15,000 kg).

TRUCKS THAT WORK

Today, trucks do many different things. Some trucks move food or clothes from warehouses or stores. Some trucks carry gasoline for other vehicles to use. Other trucks have special jobs.

Garbage trucks carry garbage from homes and stores to **landfills**. These trucks help keep cities clean.

Truck drivers use special CB
radios to talk to each other.
They are like walkie-talkies.

Tow trucks pull cars that do not work. Tow trucks have flashing lights. These lights tell other drivers that the truck is towing a car.

Fire trucks also have flashing lights. They have sirens, too. Lights and sirens tell people that the truck is in a hurry. Fire trucks have water hoses and ladders. Firefighters use them to put out fires.

MOST FIRE TRUCKS ARE PAINTED BRIGHT RED

A Trucker's Life

Truck drivers are called truckers. They drive semitrailers to many places. Truckers drive miles and miles to get things to stores.

Trucks haul many things. Sometimes trucks get too heavy to be on the roads. Weigh stations are places where truckers can find out how heavy their trucks are. Truckers weigh their trucks on big scales.

Some semis are so big that
they have 18 wheels. That is
more than four cars have!

Tough dump trucks haul dirt and rocks

Truckers need a place to rest, too. There are lots of truck stops along the highways. Truck stops have spaces for the big trucks to park in. Some truck stops have places to eat at, too.

Trucks carry many things to many places. The next time you go somewhere, see how many different trucks you can find on the road!

SOME TRUCKS CARRY SODA POP TO STORES

Hands-on: Loaded Down

Trucks can carry many things, big or small. How much can your truck hold?

What You Need

A toy truck, such as a dump truck
A handful of paper clips
A handful of cotton balls
Wooden blocks

What You Do

1. Fill the truck with as many paper clips as you can. How many paper clips fit in the truck?
2. Fill the truck with cotton balls. How many cotton balls fit in the truck?
3. Fill the truck with wooden blocks. How many blocks fit in the truck? Could the truck carry more blocks, cotton balls, or paper clips?

DUMP TRUCKS ARE VERY USEFUL VEHICLES

Index

Words to Know

engineers—people who make the parts that power vehicles

gasoline—a liquid that is used to power vehicles

landfills—places where garbage is taken

license—a card that gives permission to drive on public roads

passengers—people who ride in a truck but do not drive it

Read More

Bingham, Caroline, ed. *Big Book of Trucks*. New York: DK Publishing, 1999.

Mitton, Tony. *Tough Trucks*. Boston: Kingfisher, 2005.

Priddy, Roger. *My Big Truck Book*. New York: Priddy Books / St. Martin's Press, 2003.

Explore the Web

Make a Strange Truck http://www.enchantedlearning.com/Slidetrucks/ Slidetruck.html

Roadway Express Kids http://www.roadway.com/kids/trucks.html

Tonka Truck Games www.hasbro.com/tonka